# 5-STAR MIDWEST BOOK REVIEW ...

Young readers ages 8 and up will appreciate a memoir of adventure, following Bibi and Babu (Swahili names for Grandma and Grandpa) in a color photo-enhanced read about a couple's experience traveling in Tanzania and Kenya.

This journal of the authors' travels is designed to be used as an attention-getting, revealing saga for a younger age group which normally receives African information only from geography treatments, and it does an excellent job of juxtaposing facts about the country with personal observations capturing the cultural contrasts of the countries: "*The soulful eyes and bright smiles of Tanzanian children remind us of an innocence lost in our fast-paced technological world of today. Yet, ironically, even in the primitive villages of the Maasai tribe, we see teenagers talking into cell phones.*"

Young readers won't anticipate this candid blend of geography and personal experience, but the observations pull no punches and succeed in capturing the realities and various nuances of modern Africa: "*In Tanzania, there are more than 20 tribal cultures living peacefully together, whereas in the countries surrounding Tanzania – from west to east, the Democratic Republic of Congo, Uganda, Rwanda, Burundi, Kenya, Zambia, Malawi and Mozambique – violent unrest and some civil wars still exist. We got a glimpse of this before flying into Tanzania, when we had to land in Nairobi, Kenya. Its international airport had been burned days before we landed. Temporary tents and confusion spread everywhere.*" Add question-and-answer sessions designed to make kids observe and think and you have even more added value than a typical travel story alone would offer.

Packed with color photos of wildlife and people on every page, Bibi & Babu in Africa provides a rare exposè capturing Africa's world in just under sixty pages for an age group that rarely receives a traveler's view of Tanzania and Kenya, and is a lively, educational, and fun leisure read all in one; certain to incite an interest in African peoples and cultures.

**D. DONOVAN, SENIOR REVIEWER, MIDWEST BOOK REVIEW**

# What Our Readers Say ...

BIBI & BABU IN AFRICA was entertaining, educational and beautifully documented with photos. My son, age 8, and I read it together as a bedtime story. We both enjoyed the story of Bonnie (Bibi) and John (Babu) traveling to Africa, the animals they encountered, the people they met and the food they ate. We learned about customs, meaning of the clothes, dancing, and language of the Maasai village people. We enjoyed Bonnie telling us about the orphanage in Africa and the work she did during her visit. We also learned interesting facts about Africa's highest mountain called Mount Kilimanjaro that John climbed at 77 years-old. Amazing!

My son now dreams of going to Africa some day, but the best part, I told him, is that Bonnie and John are writing more books about new adventures they take. We can't wait to see where BIBI and BABU go next.

**Leslie Raddatz, mental health advocate and author of FLASHBACK IN POST-TRAUMATIC STRESS DISORDER: Surviving the Flood of Memories**

BIBI & BABU IN AFRICA is delightful. The authors' entertaining account of their safari adventure is accompanied by beautiful photographs. Lions, monkeys, and elephants . . . oh, my! I especially enjoyed reading about Mr. Christiansen's trek up Mt. Kilimanjaro. Bibi and Babu had a great time in Africa, and it was fun to "take" the trip with them through their story.

**Johnnie Alexander, award-winning author of WHERE TREASURE HIDES, World War II Historical Fiction**

BIBI & BABU IN AFRICA took me on an armchair vacation . . . one I don't know I'd be up to. What a brilliant book! I hung on every word and photo. Bibi and Babu are made of stern stuff . . . adventurous souls. And so are the very strong and resilient inhabitants of that region of Africa they visited. Every page came alive.

**J. Carson Black, New York Times and USA Today best selling author of crime thrillers, THE SHOP and FLIGHT 12.**

The moment I opened the first page to BIBI AND BABU IN AFRICA, I was taken on an amazing journey with authors Bonnie Toews and John Christiansen. I loved this book. The photos are stunning along with glimpses into the lives of the Maasai people. I felt as if Bonnie and John were my tour guides through the Serengeti, where we saw lions, graceful giraffes, elephants, and other wildlife.

The section on the orphanage is especially moving. I highly recommend the entire series. Homeschoolers, libraries, children's groups, and schools should all acquire copies of 'Bibi and Babu in Africa'. I'm looking forward to reading the rest of the series.

**Rita Gerlach, Author of the DAUGHTERS OF THE POTOMAC series**

# BONNIE TOEWS & JOHN CHRISTIANSEN

# BIBI & BABU

## *in Africa*

### VOLUME 1

## WHISTLER HOUSE PUBLISHING

AN IMPRINT OF SIGNALMAN PUBLISHING
U.S.A.

Cover & Interior Design: Whistler House Publishing
Photos: © John Christiansen
Cover Photo of Bonnie and John: © Annette Christiansen Walker
Editor: Bonnie Toews
Photos of terrorists' attacks in Kenya © www.mirror.co.uk and © ivanfjeld
Black Rhino © Buddymays | Dreamstime.com
Family of Cheetahs © Julianwphoto | Dreamstime.com
Defensive Puff Adder © Ecophoto | Dreamstime.com
Eating Pink Flamnigos © Mordan80 | Dreamstime.com
Lion © 2013 Regina Moses

## REFERENCES & ACKNOWLEDGEMENT:
1. Mlola, Gervase Tatah. The Ways of the Tribe—A Cultural Journey Across North-Eastern Tanzania, E & D Vision Publishing, 2010.
2. Pons, Alain. Wild Tanzania, Tanganyika Wildlife Safari.

### *Library of Congress Cataloguing-in-Publication Data*

*Toews, Bonnie and Christiansen, John*
   *Bibi & Babu in Africa: Volume 1/Bonnie Toews and John Christiansen*
   *ISBN-13: 978-1-940145-46-4*
   *LCCN: 2015942322*
1.   *Travel Series: Volumes 1-5*
   *8.5 in. x 11 in. (21.59 cm x 27.94 cm) 4-color on white paper*

**Published by Whistler House Publishing**
**An Imprint of SIGNALMAN PUBLISHING**
**Order Sales & Distribution: John McClure**
**Email: john@signalmanpublishing.com**
**Phone: 1-888-907-4423**

**This is not a guide book for tourists.**
**It is a journal of the authors'**
**travel experiences and impressions**
**for those who want to explore**
**beyond the shores of their own worlds**
**and live their own dreams.**
**Ten per cent of the royalties**
**earned by this book is**
**dedicated to the Kilimanjaro Orphanage**
**Center in Moshi, Tanzania**

**Printed in the United States of America.**

Dedicated to our grandchildren
Jesse, Amanda & Megan
Jessica & Ryan
Daniel & Ethan


With special acknowledgement
to the children of the
Kilimanjaro Orphanage Centre
who touched our hearts forever

6

# BIBI & BABU IN AFRICA
## with Bonnie Toews and John Christiansen

Africa is a land of enchantment, and Tanzania best represents life in Africa as it was long ago. About 946,000 square kilometres in size, vast plains, huge lakes and high mountains make up this country's landscape.

In the well-protected parks of Tanzania, it is possible to watch Africa's magnificent wild life roaming free and to re-unite with nature as it was meant to be, unspoiled by hunters or poachers who kill elephants, for instance, to steal and sell their ivory tusks.

Here we meet simple, loving, peaceful people with no apparent racial bias. The soulful eyes and bright smiles of Tanzanian children remind us of an innocence lost in our fast-paced technological world of today. Yet, ironically, even in the primitive villages of the Maasai tribe, we see teenagers talking into cell phones.

In Tanzania, there are more than 20 tribal cultures living peacefully together, whereas in the countries surrounding Tanzania – from west to east, the Democratic Republic of Congo, Uganda, Rwanda, Burundi, Kenya, Zambia, Malawi and Mozambique – violent unrest and some civil wars still exist.

We got a glimpse of this before flying into Tanzania, when we had to land in Nairobi, Kenya. Its international airport had been burned days before we landed. Temporary tents and confusion spread everywhere, and we almost didn't make our connecting flight to the Kilimanjaro International Airport at Arusha in Tanzania.

On our return trip to Canada, we again landed at the airport in Nairobi, which had been restored to efficient service, and took off just hours before a major terrorist attack began at the Westgate Shopping Mall in Nairobi (September 21, 2013). The siege lasted three days; 67 people were killed and 200 wounded. The attackers could just have easily made the airport their target but, because of the fire weeks before, security at the airport was on high alert.

*For us at home, the only wild animals from Africa we see are those who have been captured and imprisoned in zoos or trained to be circus performers.*

This is why it is easy to understand how, with its peaceful ways, Tanzania has become the mecca for international tourism in Central Africa. You can either travel on safaris to see wildlife in its natural habitat, test your physical limits and climb the second highest mountain in the world – Mount Kilimanjaro – or laze on beaches along the Indian Ocean on the country's eastern shores.

*John points to the peak of Mount Kilimanjaro at the beginning of his "dream-come-true" climb.*

*As seen through the front window of our guide's Land Rover, the Chinese have invested in building super highways in Tanzania.*

While there are freshly paved highways provided by Chinese investors on the main routes between Arusha and Moshi, the safari trails and routes off the main highways are rocky, pitted gravel roads. We understand why Toyota Land Rovers, Land Cruisers and Mini-Buses are the people's main choices of vehicle. Somehow they withstand the terrible abuse suffered from the constant bone-jarring bumping and rocking at top speed – which our guides call the "African massage" – over these neglected roads.

# PREPARING FOR OUR AFRICAN SAFARI

*Arriving at our hotel's outside
lobby,* **The Outpost,** *we are
issued keys to our cottage.*

*The pathway to our cottage.*

After landing at the
Kilimanjaro International
Airport in Arusha, Tanzania,
our driver guide – *DEO* – from
G Adventures Tours met us
to take us to our hotel, **The
Outpost** in Arusha. From
the start, Deo nicknamed
us **Bibi** and **Babu** (grandma
and grandpa in Swahili),
and he took the best care of
us throughout our camping
safari. Our tour director –
*Patrick Madafaa* – joined us at
the hotel that evening for our
group's briefing. There were
12 of us. Patrick too became
extended family. The next day
we began our extraordinary
safari.

*Our bedroom suite.*

# On our first day . . .

we traveled through Arusha's suburbs . . .

. . . on our way to the village of a **Maasai** tribe just outside of Arusha at **Mosquito River.** A young Maasai woman escorted us over the rice paddies clogging the river to the village on the other side where we saw thatched huts held together with cow dung in the same way as mortar binds bricks.

In the Mosquito River village, Maasai children followed our group everywhere.

*Stefanie Wyss and Regina Moses from Bern, Switzerland, play with the children.*

During our village tour, Babu had fun stirring the tribe's banana beer. He even tasted it. "Not bad," he said.

# At Mosquito River . . .

we learned how the Maasai people make their souvenirs . . .

. . . while our tour director Patrick talked to one of the Maasai artists.

## Who are the Maasai?

*The Maasai are a tribe of people who live in parts of Tanzania and Kenya who were once feared to be head hunters. They are tall and fierce warriors recognized by the special red cloth they wear that's called a* **shuka.** *Maasai people live a nomadic life, which means they move from place to place with their animals.*

# NGORONGORA NATIONAL PARK

A Primitive Maasai Village

The next morning we visited another Maasai village in the heart of the Ngorongora National Park. Here we saw how the people have retained their aboriginal way of life.

Around 1700, the Maasai migrated from the Sudan to Tanzania. They were looking for better grazing land for their cattle.

The Maasai live inside thorned enclosures called a **boma**. Each boma contains huts made of sticks, grass and cow dung mixed with ash. Straw dome-like roofs cover the huts. Animal pens fence in each hut. From time to time, the women smear cow dung on the walls of the huts to prevent leaks.

Inside, each hut is split into a small kitchen, which contains an earthen fireplace and a wood bed where the children sleep, and one bedroom for the mother. Often the children sleep with her. Leading to the outside is a narrow hall where lambs and young goats are sheltered and there are shelves to store food and firewood.

Maasai men have many wives. This is more to ensure the tribe's survival than for prestige. When a man chooses a wife, her father pays him in cattle to enlarge his herd. The men measure their wealth by the number of cattle they own. Maasai women must build and repair the huts their families live in, fetch water, collect firewood, milk cows and take care of the children. When there are two or three wives in the household, the work is shared.

Maasai warriors wear red and brown **rubega**, a cloak that hangs from their shoulders, while the women wear a longer garment dyed more modestly in colours of black and blue as well as deep red. Both men and women traditionally pierce their ears and adorn themselves with beaded necklaces and brass wire.

Here Babu wears the rubega as he joins the warriors in the welcome dance for our tour group. When the young men jump into the air, they seem to hang suspended as if they are trying to reach the sky.

Fascinated with the way the tribe lived, Babu asked so many curious questions that he gave the elders a greater chance to talk and show what they do.

Two things happened: the Maasai are a proud people and he made them feel good about themselves and how they live, and our tour group learned so much more about the Maasai. As is their custom, the elder offered the visitors a drink of fresh cow's milk. No one in the tour group volunteered to drink it because it is unpasteurized, except Babu. After he swished down the milk and pronounced it, "*Good,*" he then extended his hand in a gesture he wanted more, the tour guide's eyes popped in delight. It was the first time he had seen a westerner return the Maasai's hospitality according to their custom.

After the men performed their ritual welcome, the women invited some of us to join them in the customary shaking of their shoulders in rhythm to the beat of the song the men sing.

The Maasai speak the **Maa** language. On average, they are tall, slender people, courageous and military in posture. It is estimated their national population in Tanzania is about 600,000. Their central diet is meat, milk and blood from cattle for protein and caloric needs, which is why they were called savages by early explorers. In fact, the Maasai do not like meat that has not been killed from within their own herd. They do not hunt the wild animals roaming their grasslands and plains. This "live and let live" attitude of the Maasai is why Tanzanian game sanctuaries are so successful. In the Ngorongoro Conservation Area, for instance, about 52,000 Maasai live with their livestock together with the nearly 40,000 wild animals and birds found there.

*Village Puppy*

*The children in this village are adorable, but are very shy of strangers.*

**Maasai** artwork is based on their **culture**, which is contempt for pain, mastery of the body and the soul, control of the instincts and a rare courage needed to confront the wild animals sharing their territory. It was amazing to watch Maasai boys walk across the savannah only carrying spears and sticks. Our guide Deo explained that after a Maasai warrior slayed a lion, lions of today recognize the Maasai shadow and will never risk facing one of their warriors in battle again.

*Babu bartered with young Maasai warriors for more souvenirs.*

SAMPLES OF MAASAI ARTWORK

# Bibi & Babu's Vow of Love . . .

At the end, life is like quicksand and passes in a moment. Babu and I had already experienced this with the death of our spouses. Both had long-term illnesses that required our dedicated caregiving. Every day we were robbed of the person we knew and loved. Every day we grieved over every new loss of their dignity, independence and vitality. Every day we smiled brightly while our hearts and souls were tortured with their pain in our prison of helplessness to relieve their suffering. When that final moment came, we welcomed it with relief for they were finally free to fly with the angels.

But then came the realization that we were really alone, and life seemed empty. I know I looked in the mirror, and as the TV star Betty White loves to tell the audience, I didn't know who that person was because I still felt twenty-one in spirit. Babu's epiphany was similar as we both declared on our own, "I want to live!"

In that exclamation of the soul, we released the past and welcomed the future.

Very soon after, I stopped at a Tim Horton's Donut Shop and ahead of me in line was Babu. When he turned around, his twinkle disarmed me and within seconds we were chatting away like old friends. I really had an appointment that I wished I didn't have to keep, but as I was unlocking my car door, Babu came dashing out the Tim Horton's door calling, "I have to give you a hug."

My heart lifted. And when he hugged me, I felt as if I had come home. "We're going to see each other again, aren't we?" he said.

"OH YES," I sighed, and handed him my personal business card.

Is there a simple beginning to every love story? I don't know. But, from the outset, we felt free in spirit ... together. We intuitively trusted each other and could talk abut anything without feeling judged or embarrassed. We laughed at the silliest of things because as Babu likes to say, "Life is too serious to be serious."

We dared to dream. Babu had

# in Tanzanite and Diamonds under Maasai Magic

always wanted to climb Mount Kilimanjaro in Africa, and I had wanted to return to Africa after being in Rwanda in 1994. While there, I discovered a spiritual awakening that nothing had equalled since. I needed to go back, to see if that experience was one moment in time or something more significant.

Babu was 77-years-old and I was 72, but that did not give me any qualms for either of us. We decided to live our dreams, for we are what we believe we are. Besides, Babu was perfectly fit. I knew he could do it, but since I didn't have the stamina, I would cheer him on rather than hold him back. For me, going on this safari together was an adventure I never expected to enjoy in my lifetime.

And so it was here just after we left the village that we were introduced to **_tanzanite_**, which is only found and mined on Maasai land in the foothills of Mount Kilimanjaro in Tanzania. Tanzanite is actually a blue ziosite better known as a "blue diamond" because of its brilliance and fire. The more

intense the blue color is, the better the quality and the higher in value the Tanzanite stone is. With only a few years of mining left, Tanzanite is a disappearing exquisite blue stone 1,000 times rarer than diamonds with a hardness similar to emeralds.

At a trading post outside the Maasai village, Babu spent time watching the Maasai artisan grind down both tanzanite stones and diamonds. Beside his station was the entrance to a gallery of rings and jewelery. Babu pulled me inside and told me to look at the diamond and tanzanite rings.

Aside from the tanzanite's rarity and "blue chip" investment opportunity, what fascinated us even more was hearing the story about its many mystical and healing powers.

The Maasai believe tanzanite is a gemstone that shows us a graceful, gracious way to live as it uplifts and opens our hearts. It is said people who wear it feel a spiritual power pulling them up. It also encourages the wearer to help others because it helps us realize our own individual truth is connected to eternal truths. We become well-grounded in truth, nature and spirituality. While wearing tanzanite, it is also said it helps us speak our highest truth while it enhances our psychic abilities.

In the spirit of the story, Babu took my hand and said, "Things happen for a reason. This has been our truth from the first moment we met. I want you to choose a ring that represents our love for the rest of our lives together."

It seemed so right, but the price tags gnawed at my Scottish conscience. Without missing a beat, Babu said, "We're investing in our future together, aren't we?"

The clerk pulled out a different tray, and immediately I saw the ring that represented us. Three trillium tanzanite gems with a diamond set between them. The points of each gemstone represented the mountains of life we were climbing together at the same time as the three tanzanite stones spelled out our vow, "I love you." Each diamond between stood for us, **Bibi & Babu**, joined by our resilience.

# Our Nightly Camp Life

One night a giraffe came to visit our camp. We also heard lions roar and hyenas whoop near our tent while we tried to sleep. At one point I felt something pin the tent against my thigh. It reminded me of my huge Maine Coon cat who liked to stretch out beside me in bed and I actually slept peacefully.

Every meal was served in the same way with little variation from a lentil soup, rice, salads and some sort of stew followed by a choice of two desserts and GOOD coffee.

# EXPLORING SERENGETI NATIONAL PARK

After visiting the Maasai village, we spent the next two days exploring Serengeti National Park, which gets its name from the Maasai's word for "endless plains." It is Tanzania's largest national park and one of the world's best known wildlife sanctuaries. We travelled from an endless plain to a few shrubs at the foot of the hills.

During the next two days, we saw every animal except the rhinocerus, which is endangered in Tanzania. Today there are only 50 black rhinos remaining alive in Tanzania and each one is assigned a ranger to protect it from illegal poachers.

On entering the park, we were greeted by baboons and blue monkeys who entertained us by the roadside.

Newborn babies as well as older offspring clung to their mothers. The blue monkey's baby was so small we almost missed seeing it.

# Next we saw elegant giraffes.

Giraffes are browsers. On these plains, they eat leaves high up in the acacia trees or buds on shrubs. Their shoulder height is between 8 to 12 feet, and they weigh from more than 1,200 lbs. to 4,200 lbs. A giraffe eats about four per cent of its body weight daily and only drinks about 2 gallons of water per week. Like camels, they can go weeks without water as well.

# And we found our lion king.

## Don't you just want to hug him?

## Saving lions from extinction.

In 1962, disease ran rampant through the lion population in Serengeti until only 15 lions were left. Since then, research programs have been established to better understand the way the park's ecosystems work.

Along with lions, different teams of scientists study wildebeest, zebras, cheetahs and wild dogs (jackals). Selected animals are captured so researchers can collar them. Electronic devices that allow the scientists to track the animals are inserted inside their collars. This lion is one that is being monitored.

Today, scientists have determined there are 25 to 45 lions of reproductive age living in an area of about 250 square kilometres in the Serengeti sanctuary. Within each pride, lionesses come into season at the same time so that all the baby lions are born at once.

# While papa lay asleep under a roadside tree . . .

## mama kept watch.

# The lions' pride of cubs.

We could almost reach out the window of our Land Cruiser to touch these cubs.

(prides) to protect and females to mate. The females remain in their prides for life.

A pride usually consists of two to nine females with their offspring along with two to six males. Larger groups of lions with related males ensure a higher rate of survival amongst their cubs, as the males chase away competing lions. Only the males in the pride can mate with the females. Resident males are never from the same pride as their offspring. Young males are forced to leave their prides at four years of age to find new families

# A lioness and leopard on lookout for prey.

**Gazelles** are the prey of lions, cheetahs, leapards, hyenas and jackals. We marvelled at the markings of these gazelles.

Our two photos of these gazelles turned out like paintings.

We followed this leopard as he stalked a gazelle.

Further on, we saw two leopards resting in an acacia tree after eating their kill. If you look closely, you can see the remaining bone and the barely visible tail of the second leopard higher up the branch.

# A cousin of the gazelle, the impala.

*A baby impala is also easy prey for predators like cheetahs who can outrun them.*

Gazelles and impalas are two of eight species of antelope in central Africa. Both have amazing speed and agility to dodge predators like a cheetah. The impala can run at 60 km/h in a zig-zag pattern, while a gazelle can reach a sustained speed of 48 km/h. and bounds in huge leaps called *stotting* or *pronking* as it runs from its pursuer. Both an adult male impala and gazelle can grow to 75 kg. What amazed us is how nimble these beautiful creatures are.

## Black and White Rhinos.

The rhinoceros is a large, primitive-looking mammal that dates back to the Miocene era millions of years ago. In Africa, there are two species: the black and white rhinos. The black or hook-lipped rhino in the Serengeti National Park has three toes on each foot and has a thick, hairless, gray hide. The white rhino, also gray, has a pronounced hump on its neck and a long face and lives in South Africa among water holes, mud wallows and shade trees. To protect the black rhino, we were told one ranger is assigned to each rhino to protect it from poachers.

## Did you know?

*The rhino is prized for its horn, especially in Asia where it is used to make medicine and ornamental carvings. Not a true horn, it is made of thickly matted hair that bulges from the skull without skeletal support in double humps. The longer horn sits at the front of the nose.*

# Next came the elephants.

Demand for ivory has increased poaching, and the killing of elephant herds for black market profit threatens these humble giants with extinction. Tanzania's elephant population fell from around 109,000 in 2009 to about 70,000 in 2012, according to the Tanzania Elephant Protection Society.

Around 30 elephants are killed for their ivory every day, almost 11,000 each year. Tanzania has lost more elephants than any other African country, and it is feared the remaining elephant population could be wiped out within the next seven years. This is heart-breaking to hear for we don't believe there is a more noble, family-oriented animal.

In the Serengeti National Park, however, elephants and rhinos, who are even closer to utter extinction, are now protected.

This wasn't true in 1990. Then illegal poaching had reduced the park's elephant population to just 500. By 2013, the number of elephants had risen to 2,100, but in 2014 elephants were again found slaughtered.

## Did you know?

*1. The average elephant weighs from 6,600 to 11,000 lbs That equals as much weight as either four cars or four SUVs bound together would total.*
*2. In the wild, elephants can live up to 70 years. Highly intelligent, they use all senses.*

# Mother Cheetah and her Babies.

Like leopards, cheetahs and their offspring climb up acacia trees like the one below to spot gazelles as they migrate across the plain. The acacia shades them from the hot sun like an umbrella, Once the cheetah spots her prey, she stalks it until she makes a successful kill; then she carries the body of the gazelle and hauls it into the tree where she shares the meal with her cubs. Our camera batteries ran out so we did not catch all of this sequence.

## The Acacia Tree.

Like Canada's maple leaf tree, the Acacia is a "thorn" tree only found in tropical climates such as Africa. The chest that carried Moses' Ten Commandments, the **Ark of the Covenant**, is said to be made of acacia wood.

# Early sightings in September of the great migration that swarms the Serengeti plains every November and December.

*Here the wildebeest and zebras travel together – also unprotected clusters of gazelles can be seen wandering along with them*

The grasslands produce high-quality nutrients – unequalled anywhere else in the world – necessary for the survival of the vast herds that cross it. The cyclic shifts from dry seasons, annual bushfires and the constant trampling and grazing on the savannahs to prolonged rainy seasons has contributed to the breathtaking mass migration of the wildebeest, gazelles and zebras. Their trek begins in May-June every year. As the treeless plains dry out and whither, the wildebeest lead the herds of herbivores from the south east to the north west towards Lake Victoria passing through Serengeti in November and December after the rainy season, when the grass is rich and green and the endless pastureland is budding with flowers. This is one pattern of nature man has left uninterrupted for centuries though scientists conduct systematic studies of the Serengeti's seasonal movement. Because the plains are treeless, no giraffes participate in the migration because they cannot find the leaves and thorns on which they feed. Instead, they seek the rocky bush lands of the lower hills.

For the remaining time we spent driving through the Serengeti National Park, we saw many other animals, birds, and vegetation native to the plains.

# Zebras.

The zebras were just as curious about the tourists with their cameras pointed at them, as the people were watching them. It's amazing no one has tried to domesticate them into riding horses. They are truly beautiful and the markings on every zebra is unique. There are no clones.

# Hippos and Buffalo.

*Hippos bathing themselves. Their smell is terrible.*

*Babu holding buffalo antlers. They were so heavy, few in our safari group could lift them.*

# Fanged Snakes.

### Green Mambo

The green mamba snake is very poisonous and just as dangerous as a cobra. Its head is described as coffin-shaped. Adults are 6 to 8 feet long and live from 12 to 20 years. If startled, it will climb the nearest tree and disappear among the leaves.

### Cobra

A cousin of the green mamba, the cobra spreads out its hood when it feels angry or threatened and lifts its head high off the ground. It too is very deadly.

### Puff Adder

The puff adder is a huge and very strong snake, yet strikes with lightning speed. It is the most dangerous for tourists, because it blends with the ground as it sits in the grass waiting to ambush its prey. You have to watch where you are walking at all times.

# Birds.

### *Egret*

### *Stork*

### *Hoopee*

### *Vulture*

# The Infamous Baobab Tree.

Known as the *"tree of life,"* the baobab's swollen trunk can store as much as 31,700 gallons of water. This African tree can grow up to 82 feet tall and live for several thousands of years.

**Do you think the crocodile is laughing at the odd shape of the baobab tree?**

**Nile Crocodile.**

# Can you pick the African Antelope, Jackal, Wart Hogs, Hyena, Rhodent and Monitor Lizard?

*(See the answers below.)*

**Answers:**

1. Wart Hogs
2. Monitor Lizard
3. Rhodent
4. Antelope
5. Jackal
6. Hyena

# SAFARI ENDS AT THE NGORONGORO CRATER.

This region is referred to as the ***Seat of Early Civilization, Cradle of Life*** or ***the Garden of Eden.*** From here, species of humans migrated to all points of the earth.

The crater is the remains of a volcano that exploded and collapsed on itself 2 to 3 million years ago. and is 2,000 feet deep. Its floor covers 100 square miles and measures about 12 miles wide.

We first saw it from an outlook perched on the crater's rim. At the base, seen in the distance, was ***Lake Magadi***, a soda lake. Formed more than two million years ago, its shallow waters have provided a home for thousands of birds.

We saw ostriches, crowned cranes, flamingos, pelicans, Egyptian geese, eagles and other birds of prey. Most striking were the flocks of pink flamingos on the shores of the lake.

Rich pastures that provide continuing life for the approximate 30,000 mammals that live here year-round carpet the crater floor. Deep slopes and highland forests surround the crater effectively containing any animals from leaving

In 1979, the Ngorongoro Crater was named a **UNESCO World Heritage Site.** The conservation area in this part of Tanzania protects wildlife while allowing human access. For example, the Maasai can graze their cattle on the rich grasslands within the crater during the day but must remove their herds at night. They are also allowed because they do not hunt the local wildlife. The bit of farming seen is only enough to feed a family. They cannot mass produce or sell what they grow.

The elevation of the crater floor is 5,900 feet above sea level. This altitude modifies the tropical temperature together with eastern trade winds that bring 31 to 47 inches of rainfall per year to the crater. As we travel through the bordering forests and along the grasslands, we can see how this is still a Garden of Eden for the wildlife living here.

On the last day of our safari we also saw the most wondrous skies and sunsets on our return drive to Arusha.

# OUR TOUR GROUP

**FROM LEFT TO RIGHT:**

BACK ROW – Kristina Otto, Oldensburg, Germany; Fabian Sobotka, Bremen, Germany.

SECOND ROW – Anna and her daughter Bree Stadelmann, Dawson Creek, British Columbia, Canada; Lindsay Borden, Toronto, Ontario, Canada; Ruth Harper, London, England; Bonnie Toews, Mount Albert, Ontario, Canada; Irene Jaakson, Coquitlam, British Columbia, Canada; Reiner Jaakson, Oakville, Ontario, Canada; Deo, our G-Adventure guide from Arusha, Tanzania; Stefanie Wyss, Bern, Switzerland; Regina Moser, Bern, Switzerland.

FRONT ROW: Chief cook for camping safari tour; Patrick Madafaa, G-Adventure tour director for our safari; John Christiansen, Mount Albert, Ontario, Canada.

# PART II: A DREAM FULFILLED
## The journey begins.

On the second part of our trip, Babu joined his group of eleven from Britain, Australia and Canada to start their six-day trek from September 14 to September 19 to climb Mount Kilimanjaro, the tallest peak in Africa – 19,341 feet or 5,895 metres.

Alfons, the mountain tour guide, and Babu's personal porter, Emanuel, promised me to look after "Papa" on his climb up the mountain.

At 77 years of age, Babu is the second oldest man to try and master this mountain.

**Camping on the first night.**

Each person only carries a back pack with what they need for the day's climb – water, snacks, or change in clothing.

Porters carry supplies and climbers' suitcases.

**The mountain trail.**

As the group **pole, pole** – walk slowly – to adjust to the altitude and climb, their shadows advance in front of them.

**One of the toughest things on the climb was stepping over huge boulders.**

Babu's tour guide Alfons pauses to put on his sunglasses. The higher you climb, the more radiant the sun is, and it can be quite harmful.

**More boulders to climb over.**

# Glaciers and Shadows

Looking back down to camp.

**This picture shows Babu on the last lap of his climb to the peak of Mount Kilimanjaro at sunrise.**

The group was awakened at midnight to climb this segment so they could arrive at the mountain peak as the sun rose. From here, Babu could see the earth's curvature on the distant horizon. It reminded him we live on a planet in the midst of a vast and amazing universe.

# *Reaching the peak . . .*

## *19,341 feet or 5,895 metres high.*

**Babu and his porter at the top of Mount Kilimanjaro.**

On the last leg of his climb, Emanuel carried Babu's backpack to make sure he would put most of his strength into climbing rather than in carrying the extra weight on his back. Behind them are the mountain's glaciers.

The porters and guides escort tours every two weeks. They are amazingly strong and have adapted to the rigors of Mount Kilimanjaro. When one young girl collapsed, her porter carried her on his back down the mountain to the ambulance waiting at the gate.

# The Achievement!
## September 18, 2013

The porters told Babu, at 77 years old, he is the second oldest man to climb Mount Kilimanjaro. The record holder is 84.

His picture is taken here with some of the members of his group who made it to the top. Babu is in the yellow jacket, balaclava and sunglasses. At the peak, it is freezing cold, between 0 to -10 degrees Fahrenheit, and the wind can be brutal. If climbers do not dress properly, they suffer from frostbite and hypothermia. For Babu's group, there was no wind that morning, and they saw the true glory of the mountain peak.

# The way back down... even tougher.

Meanwhile, as I waited for Babu to complete his climb, I could see the sun set on Mount Kilimanjaro on the same night as Babu reached the summit the next morning. It was the only night through the week when the mountain was visible from our Springlands Hotel room in Moshi, and I knew he would reach the top, just as he wanted to do. But, it was even worse waiting for him to come down. His endurance test was not yet over.

**The original conquerer.**

**The 2013 conquerers.**

After the group had successfully climbed Mount Kilimanjaro, a picture was taken at the park gate. By now, Babu had lost ten pounds, and when he dismounted the shuttle back at the hotel, I was greeted with a wild-looking, gaunt man. He had not bathed or shaved in six days, but he had conquered his mountain! And it was NOT a cat walk.

I was SO proud of him, as were all our families, including those in Germany. Few people have Babu's fierce determination, stamina, good health, self-confidence and vision to achieve their dreams.

# PART III: OUR VISIT AT THE ORPHANAGE

## Together again, Babu and I have one last thing to do before we leave Tanzania.

We both love children, and the children in Africa are unique in many ways. They illustrate lost innocence at the same time as they endure some of humankind's most brutal and primitive treatment.

While Babu was climbing Mount Kilimanjaro, I had found an orphanage just five minutes from our hotel. During the week I had volunteered to help with another Canadian volunteer, Karolina Nieszczerzewicz from Windsor, Ontario. She dedicated her three-week holiday to work 10-hour days at the orphanage. She and I connected on a spiritual level, and on his return, Babu eagerly looked forward to interacting with the children as well.

**KILIMANJARO ORPHANAGE CENTRE IN PASUA, TANZANIA, IN 2013.**

My hostess, seventeen-year-old Agness Athumani, stays to help look after the younger children. This picture is taken in one of the girls' dorm rooms, which has two sets of bunk beds three tiers high. Two children sleep in each bunk. Not surprising. The girls' rooms were much neater than the boys. I was pleased to see their mattresses were made of foam, so comfortable and supportive for their young bodies. You'll notice mosquito netting attached to each bunk as well. Malaria-carrying mosquitos are a constant threat to children in Tanzania. Both of our guide's boys – six months and three years old – were taken to hospital with malaria while he was on tour with us.

The cook for the orphanage works in a very primitive kitchen with a concrete countertop over a bricked-in wood stove. The children's diet is mainly rice and maize. I saw no evidence of milk served. Older girls like Agnes walk to a well one mile away every morning to carry back pails of water balanced on their heads for the day's supply. The children have no hot water for bathing and cleaning and have to wash their laundry by hand.

The shock for me was seeing how the dishes are washed. I helped pile dirty plates, pots and utensils into one huge pot. Two-gallon cans are filled with cold water. Using a bar of soap and one scraper, the washer dumps the plates and cups into the first can, scrubs them and then rinses each dish in the cold water in the can next to it. Then they are piled in another huge pot to air dry.

I can only surmise that the children's immune systems are extremely strong to tolerate such primitive cleaning methods.

**If we could help them set up a more efficient and clean way to wash their dishes, that would be a miracle I am sure they would welcome.**

Windsor's Karolina Nieszczerzewicz worked with the children for three weeks, and they loved her. Here she is with them in the only classroom. They have one old computer and one TV. At the back is a huge cupboard filled with old donated story books and readers.

The children taught us to say:
Hello – **JAMBO**
Thanks – **SANTE**
OK – **DEO**
Slowly, slowly – **POLE POLE**

Helping this orphanage has become Karolina's mission, and I understand why.

These children are gentle. They have nothing and appreciate everything. They share whatever they are given. They like to stroke your hair, to listen to music, to dance – Karolina calls it getting their endorphins moving.

**This is one of the rooms in the boys' dorm. Often the children only have one toy, and rather than fight over it, they share it happily.**

While I was there, parents who could not care for their six-month-old disabled baby dropped him off at the orphanage's gate. One of the younger girls picked him up and began soothing him. This often happens. The children have learned to look after themselves.

**Orphan puppy who also lives here.**

In 2013, when Aziza was 16-years-old (in picture to the left), she was one of four children American Dr. Gregory Higgins from Alaska sent to India to receive life-saving heart surgery. Without his help, Aziza would have died. She is learning English and working hard to get a good education so she can make an independent life for herself.

Like Agness, Aziza wants to return to give help to the orphanage, which gave her a home and the surrogate family the orphans create among themselves to love.

*For part of the year, Dr. Higgins and his wife, Shannon, live in Moshi to serve the orphanage directly. He has also founded a non-profit organization to help support it.*

*To help Dr. Higgins raise medical funds, GO TO:*
*http://www.kiliorphanagecentre.org/donations/4574559388*

To me, Shedrack represents the heart and soul of this orphanage. His engaging smile, perky personality, bright eyes and quick intelligence are mesmerizing. I could immediately picture him growing up to be a historical leader like Nelson Mandella. His T-shirt says it all: **THIS HEART DON'T BREAK.**

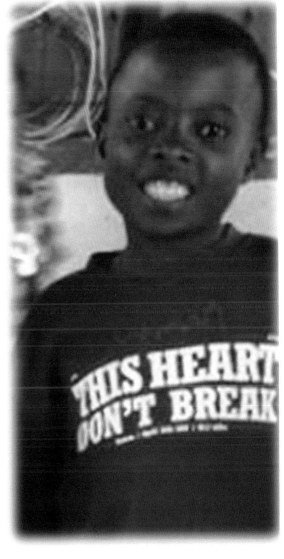

Words to haunt you because Shedrack has sickle cell anemia, but this amazing boy does not feel sorry for himself. In and out of hospitals and orphaned after his mother died, he has endured and persevered with an unexpected zest for life. Living at the orphanage has helped to stabilize his condition. Each day is a new adventure he welcomes. He loves school, and despite his illness, has passed all his national exams. No challenge is too great. I watched him master the use of our cell phones. He took amazing photos that showed me he has a director's eye for production. He is a man, an old soul, wise beyond his years and an inspiration to everyone who is blessed to know him.
### *Hoorah, Shedrack!*

In order to succeed in life, these orphan children must learn to speak English and go to school. It costs $500.00 per child to send each one to school for one year.

To prepare them I believe they need interactive games such as we have here to help children learn to speak and read English, even at two years old. These simple independent programs the children could share as they learn and improve in speaking English, which is the official language of Tanzania, along with native Swahili.

At this time, there are 52 children living in the orphanage.

**Agness has a dream – to be a dress designer and an actress. We told her if Babu could reach his dream at 77-years-old, she could reach hers too.**

The first thing the children ask you, "What is your name? How old are you?" To which I answered, "My name is Bonnie, and I am 72-years-old."

They called me Bibi for Grandma from then on. And when they met John, they called him Babu, for Grandpa.

While visiting the orphanage, Babu found himself lifting children into his arms without thinking who they were or what they might have. Some of the children are HIV-positive, and their need for love and acceptance is just as important to him as responding to any other child. He ran and played with them. And they laughed with joy because they were having fun.

Everywhere Babu went he shared the boy within himself, not just with the children, but also with the people and they along with the children responded with raised self-esteem for he made them feel proud of themselves and who they are. This is a rare humanitarian gift Babu has.

In many ways, our 16 days in Tanzania were life-changing. It was our first trip as a couple, and when we left Africa, we came away with vivid memories, new lifetime friends from all parts of the world and our souls enriched with the blessings of this extraordinary journey that we took together.

# UPDATE

As this book goes to print, two years have passed. Much has changed, for the orphanage and for us. With worldwide support, more of its goals are being met and there is new hope for the now 62 children under its care. **We are also dedicating 10% of our royalties earned by this book** to the *Kilimanjaro Orphanage Centre.*

**You can help too. To find out how, GO TO:**

*Agness has started to realize her dream. She and Aziza model headresses she creates from the fabric scraps we send her. Here Agness appears with two other girls wearing her designs, while top left is another example of Agness' stunning ideas for a headress. We are so proud of her and Aziza.*

*http://www.kiliorphanagecentre.org*
*a registered Non-Governmental Organization (Charter # 3959),*
ON FACEBOOK: *https://www.facebook.com/kiliorphanagecentre*

The mission of the Kilimanjaro Orphanage Centre is to provide food, clothing, shelter, education, spiritual guidance and medical care to the children in its care and to other local children in need.

# About the Founder and Directors

### "TEACHER" EDWARD LAZARO & DATIVA

"Teacher" Edward Lazaro represents the traditional African approach of "everyone" or the village owning their children, but this continuing HIV crisis has gone beyond the ability of the local people to care for so many children on their own. A Mt. Kilimanjaro guide, "Teacher" is the founder of the Majengo pre-school, and it is here where the abandoned children in the area gather. He and his wife, DATIVA, who teaches with him and runs the pre-school while he takes tourist up the mountain, has supported him in caring for these children. They dreamed of giving these children a home where they could feel safe and nourished, but the couple could not afford to do it on their own.

### ZAINAB ANSEL & REMMY ADAM

In 2009, his employer, Zainab Ansel (**Mama Zara**), founder and manager of Zara Tours (*www.zaratours.com*), and her sister, Remmy Adams, sponsored "Teacher's" dream to open a shelter for this ever-expanding population of orphaned children in the Kilimanjaro region. Through Zara Tours' publicity of the orphanage to mountain-climbing tourists staying at its neighboring Springland Hotel, we, for instance, would not have known about the orphanage and never had a chance to visit it. Zara Tours' support has led to a coalition of dedicated Tanzanian, American and European volunteers to manage the Kilimanjaro Orphange Centre.

### TRAVIS YOUNG

After visiting KOC in 2010, Travis from York in the United Kingdom committed to create the KOC's web site and Facebook page to promote the daily events of the orphanage and to raise awareness of its ongoing needs. He faithfully carries on this responsibility.

### HANNO BREITFUSS & UDO NEYER

From Lichtenstein, Hanno Breitfuss, a self-employed real estate developer, and Udo Neyer, have helped KOC get the land they need to expand its operation.

UNICEF estimates there are more than 3.1 million children living in Tanzania without parents. Of these, the AIDS/HIV plague has orphaned 1.2 million. Many of these orphans also live with the disease.

# In Special Service

### DR. GREG HIGGINS,

Dr. Greg Higgins, a retired Emergency Department doctor from Alaska, and his wife, Shannon, spend part of their year living near the orphanage, and the other part, they return to Alaska to raise support funds to cover their volunteer time and the medical needs of the KOC. For instance, they have flown children who required heart surgery to India. "Dr. Greg" conducts regular medical check ups of the children including blood work to detect AIDS or HIV. Along with training a medical student who, when he graduates, will become a full-time doctor for the orphanage, Dr. Greg has also enlisted the help of a local dentist to look after the dental needs of the children. You can read Dr. Greg's heart-warming blogs of the daily happenings on the KOC's web site and Facebook page.

### DANIEL SARIJORI

Daniel Sarijori originally came from a Maasai tribe in Kenya. He is qualifying to become a teacher and assists "Teacher" at his pre-school as well as at the KOC to develop a full-time educational program for the youngest children. For the older children who have to be enrolled in private schools, the KOC offers a sponsorship program on its web site where contributors engage personally with the children of their choice and pay for their school fee of $500 per year.

### LUCY

Like every Mom, the guardian angels taking care of the children can be forgotten. LUCY is the full-time Head Matron of those women who have become "mothers" to the KOC children. They keep them clean, fed, and safe while making sure they get to school . . . on time.

**BEST CARE POSSIBLE is Lucy's Motto.**

# Moving Forward

The new donated land of 40 acres means "Teacher's" Majengo Pre-school and the KOC can grow maize, beans, tomatoes, carrots and potatoes to feed the children in care. Another donation of a septic tank has been installed so now the children have learned hand-washing and basic hygiene.

Though there has been continuing progress, there is still so much more that needs to be done. As a result, 2015 marks the first year the KOC has launched a worldwide appeal for

help. While the current orphanage has increased its support from 52 children to 62 in the past two years, there are so many more abandoned children living in dire circumstances. To address this special need, the KOC has stretched its goal to raise more than $200,000 USD this year to help pay for the construction of additional dormitories and facilities to accommodate up to 140 children at both the present site and on the donated farm land. The KOC has named its fund-raising project:

## HELP BUILD OUR FUTURE

*You can become a part of these children's future by donating online at:*
*https://www.crowdrise.com/kilimanjarochallengefundraiser/fundraiser/kiliorphanagecentre*

With its new farm land, the KOC is looking to become as self-sufficient as possible by developing a fully functional farm and worldwide network of sponsors to help each child get the best education possible. To this end, KOC has also hired a full-time teacher so that the youngest children in the orphanage can begin learning English and studying to qualify for a higher education that will enable them to

become productive independent adults as Agness Athumani demonstates is possible.

The KOC's classroom would also benefit from interactive learning games in English that are found online, but to access them, the children need a supply of Microsoft tablets or Ipads to participate in today's educational environment.

*To donate new/used "tablets" or "Ipads", please send them to:*

**c/o Edward "Teacher" Lazaro,**
**Kilimanjaro Orphanage Centre**
**PO Box 8959, Moshi, Tanzania.**
**Email: teachytz@yahoo.com**

**For daily orphanage updates, GO TO:**
*Kiliorphanagecentre/blogspot.com*

Made in the USA
Lexington, KY
18 July 2017